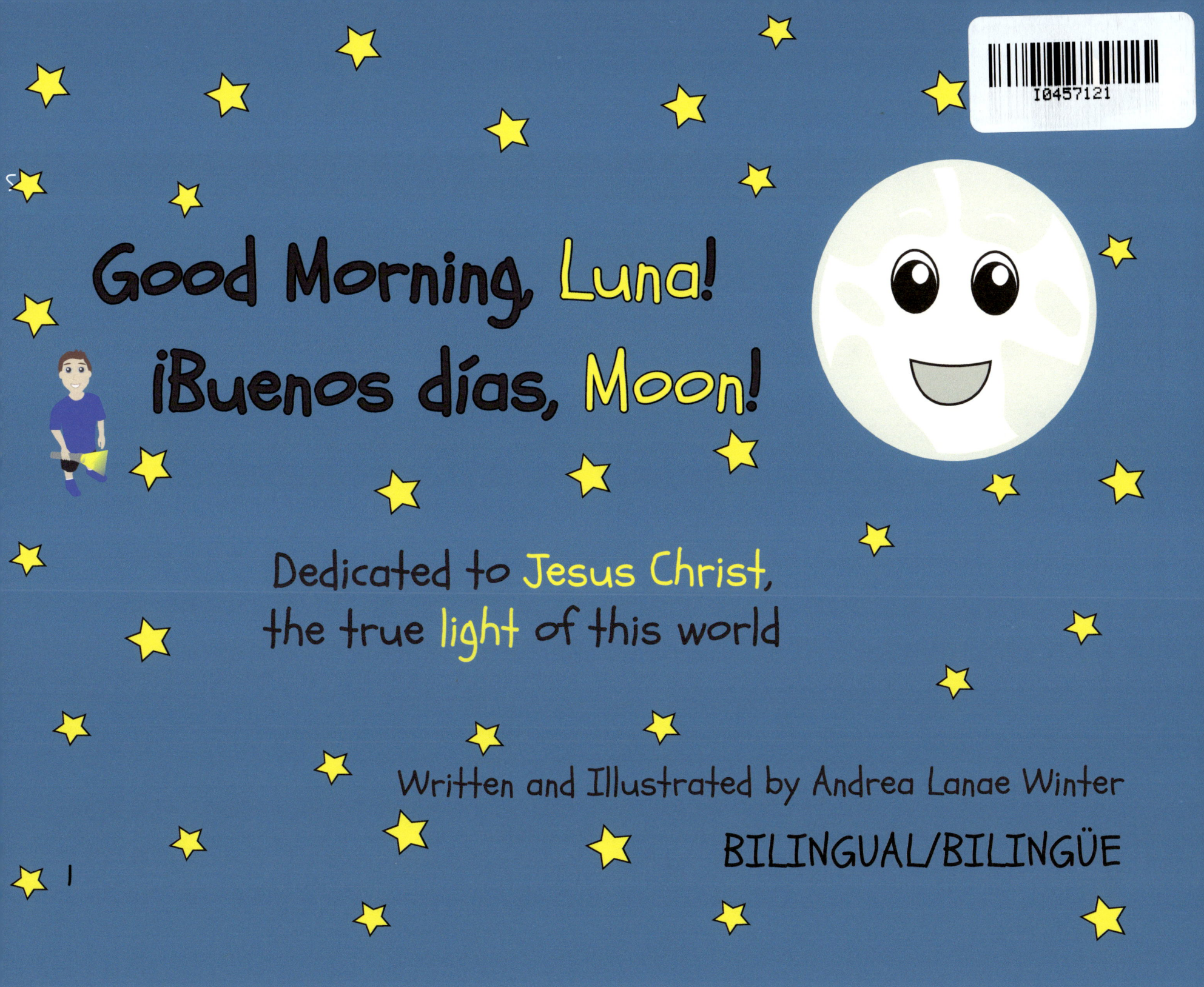

Good Morning, Luna!
¡Buenos días, Moon!

Dedicated to Jesus Christ,
the true light of this world

Written and Illustrated by Andrea Lanae Winter

BILINGUAL/BILINGÜE

Song by Yancy. Check out her "Little Praise Party" series available in both English and Spanish. Her music is everything kids love and everything adults value. Listen anywhere you stream music or learn more at YancyNotNancy.com.

Listen to this book in **English** and **Spanish** online.
Visit themulticulturalheart.com and click on the **Books/Libros** tab
or **scan** the **QR code** to locate the **interactive ebook**.
Password for paperback (original) version: Cristoeslaluz

3 layers of reading/3 niveles de lectura

1. Read as a dialogue– Have one person read the role of the moon and the other person read the role of the boy.

 moon – la luna    boy – el niño

Lean el diálogo– Una persona lee una parte de la luna y la otra persona lee la otra parte del niño.

2. Family devotional– Read the Bible verses and prayer and sing the song at the end. Discuss how to light your world.

Devocional– Lean los versículos de la Biblia, oren y canten la canción. Conversen entre sí como brillar la luz de Cristo.

3. Science fun facts– Go back and read the science fun facts and do suggested activities at your own pace.

Datos curiosos de ciencias– Lean y hagan las actividades de ciencias sugeridas a su propio ritmo.

4

Good morning, Luna, how did you sleep last night?

Buenos días, **Moon**, ¿dormiste bien anoche?

I stayed awake to watch over the night. El sol is coming up to watch over the day.

Me quedé despierta para guiar la noche. **The sun** viene para guiar el día.

Luna, what is the night like when everyone is sleeping?

Moon, ¿cómo es la noche cuando todos estamos durmiendo?

Peaceful. Beautiful. Magnificent!

Llena de paz y belleza. ¡Maravillosa!

What do you see?

¿Qué ves?

I see the stars shining brightly around me and the fireflies dancing below me.

Veo las estrellas brillando a mi alrededor y las luciérnagas bailando debajo de mí.

Did you know?

Fireflies use their lights to protect themselves.
If a frog eats a firefly, do you know what happens? (Its stomach lights up!)
What happens when you feed on God's Word? (You light up!)

6

¿Sabías que?
Las luciérnagas se protegen con su luz.
¿Qué ocurre cuando una rana come una luciérnaga? (¡Su estómago se ilumina!)
¿Qué ocurre cuando te alimentas de la Palabra de Dios? (¡Te iluminas!)

7

What do you hear?

¿Qué oyes?

I hear...

Oigo...

...crickets
singing
in the
forest,

...los grillos
cantando en
el bosque,

...tiny frogs in
Puerto Rico
called **coquí** (because they say "co-quí"),

...ranas pequeñas en
Puerto Rico que se
llaman **coquí**
(porque dicen "co-quí"),

8

...and the ocean waves.

....y las olas del océano.

9

It does...and it reaches even higher when it is closest to me and tries to give me a "high tide!"

¡Sí! Se levanta hacia arriba muy alto cuando estoy muy cerca para tratar de chocar la mano durante la marea alta.

Cool, but don't you mean a "high five?"
What is a "high tide?"

¿Qué es una marea alta?

11

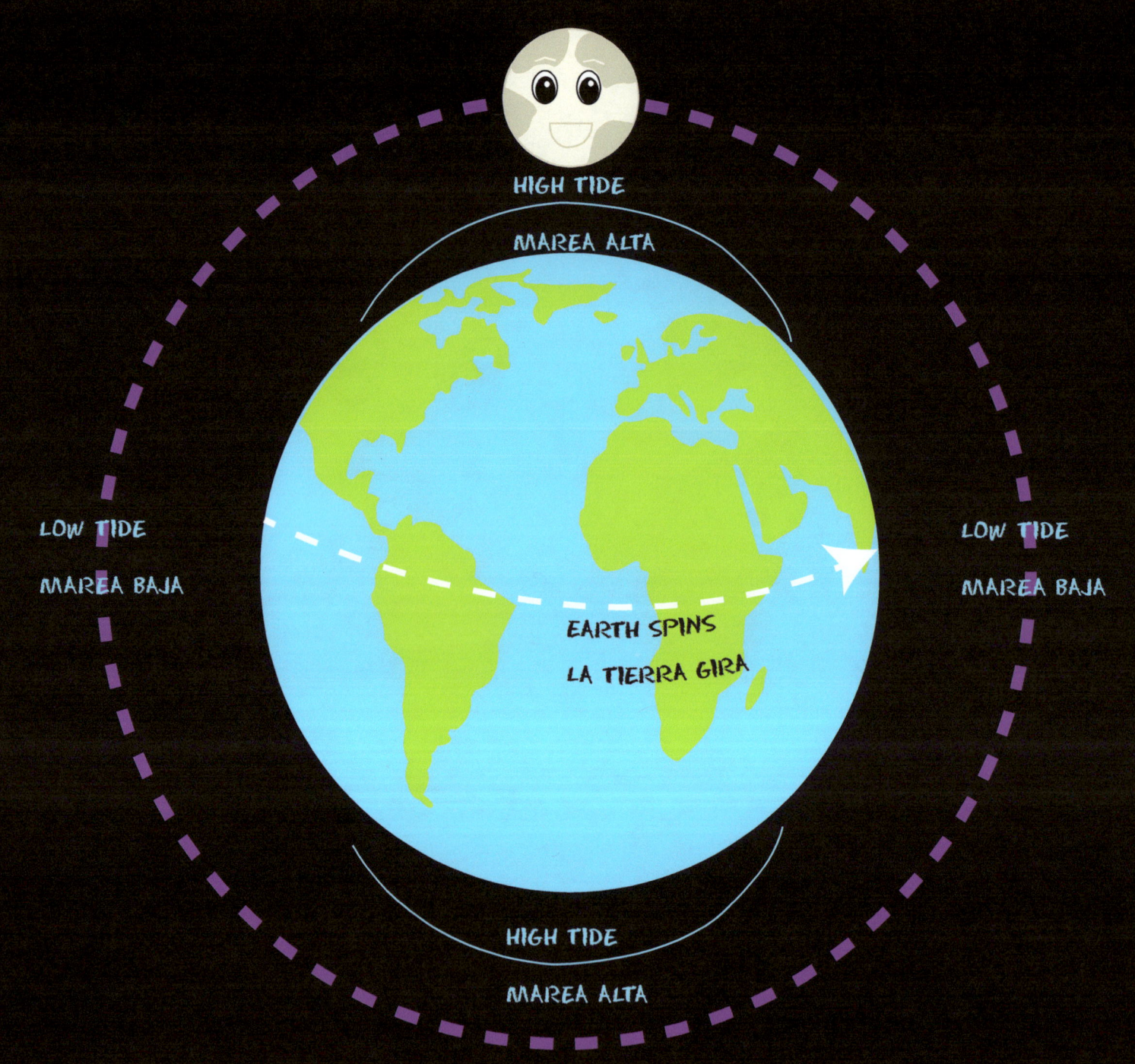

When la Tierra rotates, different sides of the Earth face me. When an ocean is facing me, my gravitational pull causes el agua to rise higher. The rising and falling of water is called a tide.

Cuando the Earth gira, sus lados me miran durante horas diferentes. Cuando un océano me mira mi fuerza gravitatoria causa que the water del océano suba. El ascenso y descenso del agua se llama una marea.

Wow! I want to ride the tide one day and reach up and give you a "high tide," Moon!

¡Guau! Yo quiero montar la marea un día y saludarte, Luna.

What else do you do at night, Luna?

¿Qué más haces por la noche, Moon?

I peek in on the adventures of the **bats** that burst out of their caves to explore the night.

Miro las aventuras de los **murciélagos** que salen rápido de sus cuevas en multitudes para explorar la noche.

COOL!

Who else is awake with you at night, Moon?

¡Qué Chévere!

¿Quién más está despierto contigo por la noche, Luna?

Did you KNOW?

Do you know how bats see at night? They cannot see with their eyes, but God gave them advanced hearing called echolocation that helps them know where they are going. What do you use to help you see at night?

¿Sabías que?

¿Sabes cómo ven los murciélagos por la noche? No ven con los ojos sino usando los oídos. Es un fenómeno que se llama ecolocación. ¿Qué usas tú para ayudarte a ver por la noche?

EL búho talks with me throughout the night.

The owl habla conmigo por la noche.

He is very wise and has lots to share!

¡Es muy sabio!

¿Sabías que?

Un búho puede girar la cabeza casi por completo.

Imagínate a este búho girando la cabeza para ver las aves azules en el árbol detrás de él.

"Whoo! Whoo!"

"uu uu"

Did you know?

Did you know that an owl can turn its head almost all of the way around?

Imagine this owl turning its head to look at the little blue birds sleeping in the tree behind it.

The nocturnal seagull also squawks "¡Hola!"

La gaviota nocturna también grazna "Hi!"

Nocturnal? What is nocturnal?

Nocturna, ¿Qué es nocturna?

Nocturnal means something that comes out at night.

Nocturna significa que algo sale por la noche.

Oh, then you are nocturnal!

¡Ah, entonces tú eres nocturna!

Fun Fact/Dato Curioso

This seagull is from the Galapagos Islands in Ecuador. Other seagulls around the world fly during the day. This seagull is nocturnal. What does "nocturnal" mean?

Esta gaviota es de las Islas Galápagos en Ecuador. Otras gaviotas en el mundo vuelan durante el día. Esta gaviota es nocturna. ¿Qué significa <<nocturna>>?

19

Baby sea turtles also come out at night. God designed my light to help these tortugas to find their way to the ocean!

Las tortugas del mar también salen por la noche. Dios diseñó mi luz para ayudar a estas turtles a encontrar su camino hacia el océano.

Your light is very important! Why do we not always see your light at night?

¡Tu luz es muy importante! ¿Por qué no siempre vemos tu luz por la noche?

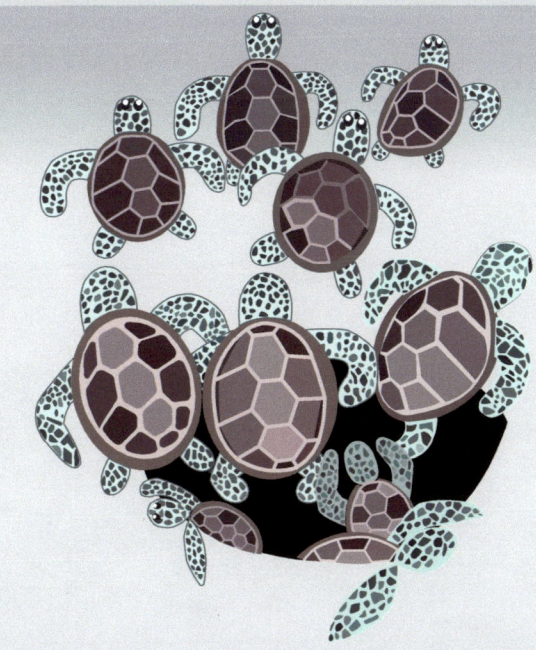

21

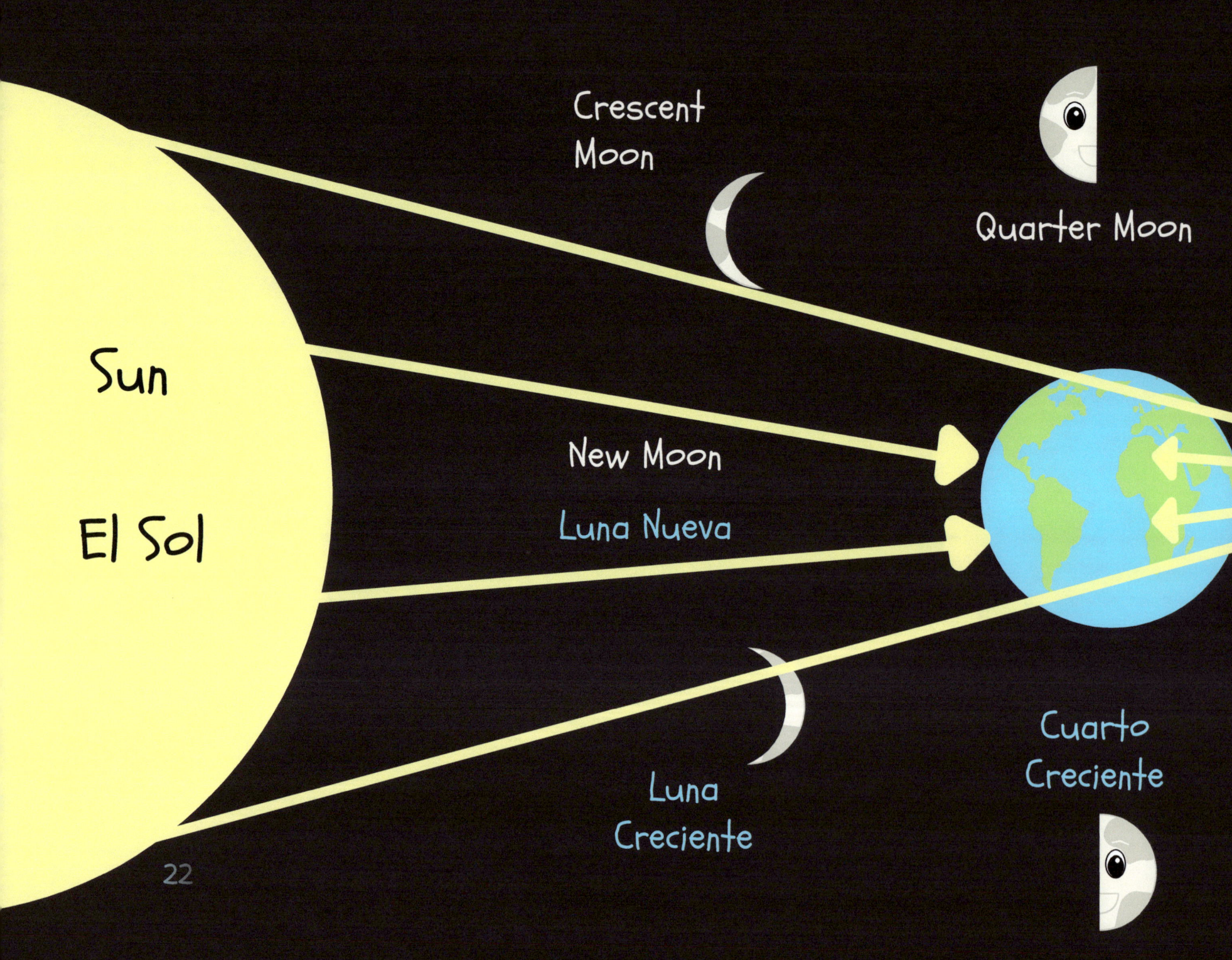

Gibbous Moon

That is a good question! Mi luz is a reflection of the sun shining on me. You can only see the part of my surface that the sun lights up!

¡Esa es buena pregunta! My light es un reflejo de la luz del sol. Solamente puedes ver la parte de la superficie que el sol me ilumina.

Full Moon

Luna Llena

FUN FACT

Did you know that when you see what appears to be half of the moon, it is really less than half? The moon is a sphere, like a ball or an orange. Try cutting an orange into four pieces. One of those slices equals one quarter or one out of four parts of the whole orange. That is how much of the moon is showing when it is a quarter moon!

DATO CURIOSO

¿Sabías que cuando ves lo que parece la mitad de la luna, de verdad es menos que la mitad? La luna es una esfera, como una pelota o una naranja. Trata de cortar una naranja en cuatro pedazos. Uno de los pedazos es un cuarto de la naranja, o uno de cuatro pedazos de la naranja. Eso es la cantidad de la luna que se ve cuando está en la fase cuarto creciente.

Gibosa Creciente

23

"Yo soy la luz del mundo. El que me sigue no andará en tinieblas, sino que tendrá la luz de la vida." –Juan 8:12 (NVI)

Jesus, the Son of God
Jesús, El Hijo de Dios

"Then Jesus said, 'I am light to the world, and those who embrace me will experience life-giving light, and they will never walk in darkness.'"

–John 8:12
(TPT)

"Porque Dios, que ordenó que la luz resplandeciera en las tinieblas, hizo brillar su luz en nuestro corazón para que conociéramos la gloria de Dios que resplandece en el rostro de Cristo." –2 Corintios 4:6 (NVI)

"For God, who said, 'Let brilliant light shine out of darkness,' is the one who has cascaded his light into us...as we gaze into the face of Jesus Christ."

–2 Corinthians 4:6 (TPT)

There is a light much brighter than the sun in this world. He is the Son of God, the true light of the world. Do you know His name?

Jesus!

Hay una luz más brillante que el sol en este mundo. Él es el Hijo de Dios, la luz verdadera del mundo. ¿Sabes cómo se llama?

¡Jesús!

25

You are the light of the WORLD
-Matt. 5:14

Yes! I see Jesus' light shining from your window. His light and love shine through you!

26

"Ustedes son la luz del mundo."

–Mateo 5:14 (NVI)

¡Sí! Veo la luz de Jesús brillando por tu ventana. ¡Su luz y amor brillan a través de ustedes!

Dear God,

Thank you for the moon.
Thank you for the way that
you made its light to be a
reflection of the sun.
Fill me with Your love as
I spend time with you so
that I reflect Your light
and love to the world.

In Jesus' name I give you
thanks,

Amen

Querido Dios,

Gracias por la luna.
Gracias por la manera
que hiciste que su luz sea
una reflexión del sol.
Lléname con Tu amor
mientras paso tiempo
contigo para reflejar Tu
luz y Tu amor al mundo.

En el nombre de Jesús te
doy gracias,

Amén

How long does it take for you to travel around the Earth, Luna?

¿Cuánto tiempo te toma para viajar alrededor de la Tierra, Moon?

A little over 27 days.

Un poco más de 27 días.

I want to travel around the world in 27 days!

¡Yo quiero viajar alrededor del mundo en 27 días!

Stay close to Jesus, and He will light your way!

Acércate a Cristo, y Él iluminará tu camino.

Gracias, Moon. See you soon!

Thank you, Luna. ¡Hasta pronto!

See you soon, Little Star! Keep letting your light shine!

¡Hasta pronto, Estrellita! ¡Sigue brillando con tu luz!

"We can all draw close to him....and...we all become like mirrors who brightly reflect the glory of the Lord Jesus."

–2 Corinthians 3:18 (TPT)

I wonder...

What does it mean to reflect the glory of Jesus?
How does the moon help us to understand this?
What do you wonder about God and His Creation?

Me pregunto...

¿Qué significa reflejar la gloria del Señor Jesús?
¿Cómo nos ayuda la luna a entender esto?
¿Qué te preguntas acerca de Dios y Su Creación?

"Así, todos nosotros, que con el rostro descubierto reflejamos como en un espejo la gloria del Señor..." –2 Corintios 3:18 (NVI)

This Little Light of Mine
(Traditional song)

This little light of mine!
I'm gonna let it shine.
This little light of mine!
I'm gonna let it shine.
This little light of mine!
I'm gonna let it shine.
Let it shine all the time.
Let it shine oh yeah.

Esta Lucecita*

Esta lucecita la dejaré brillar.
Esta lucecita la dejaré brillar.
Esta lucecita la dejaré brillar.
Brillará, brillará, brillará.

*Song by Yancy. Check out her "Little Praise Party" series available in both English and Spanish. Her music is everything kids love and everything adults value. Listen anywhere you stream music or learn more at YancyNotNancy.com.